And God Blessed
The Irish

The Story of Patrick

Library of Congress Catalog Card Number: 97-77057

ISBN: 0-9646439-6-0

Published by: Ambassador Books, Inc.
                 71 Elm Street
                 Worcester, MA 01609

To order, call: 800 577-0909

And God Blessed The Irish

The Story of Patrick

By Chris Driscoll

With Illustrations
By Susan Krikorian

Ambassador Books
Worcester, Massachusetts

Dedication

*To the Goggins and the Minnehans,
the Driscolls and the Goughs, and to
all our Irish ancestors who passed
along what Patrick gave them.*

Chapter One

Kidnapped

Things were pretty good for Patrick. His father was an important man. He and his family lived in a nice house. And Patrick had lots of friends.

His town was on a huge island called Britain, and it was very near the end of the Earth. The center of the world was a city called Rome, but that was far away, across the sea and across the mountains.

The town had a strong fort because of the wild people. Some of the wild people lived in the dark forests. And some of them lived out in the sea in a place called Ireland. Sometimes, without warning, they would attack Patrick's town.

The wild people were fierce. They had their own religion which was not like

Patrick's at all. They had magicians who did bad things. And they loved to fight and to steal.

The wild people from Ireland were very brave. They sang, and they told stories. They were big and beautiful to look at. But they were very dangerous.

Patrick did not understand the wild people. He did not know why they wanted to fight and steal. He did not understand his own people either. He did not know why they did not want to fight and steal.

He thought that God had something to do with it. But Patrick did not pay much attention to God. He had been baptized, and he had heard about Jesus. But Patrick didn't really know much about Him.

† † †

They came in the middle of the day. They were there before anybody knew it. They were screaming and cursing and fighting. There was blood and

fire and crying.

Patrick saw the wild men drag his sister away. He could not help her. He was dragged in another direction. He could smell the smoke and hear the screams and feel his fear.

It was a nightmare, but it was real. The wild people spoke strange words. They shouted at him and punched him. And they threw him in a big boat and made him row.

He stared back at the shore, shrinking in the distance. He listened to the shouts in the strange language and watched until he could no longer see his homeland. He did not cry. He showed no fear. He just rowed.

Patrick's parents were gone. His sister was gone. He felt all alone. And he knew he was alone, all alone, except for the wild people.

† † †

The wind was raw, and the rain was icy. There was no one to comfort Patrick. There was no one to love him. There was no one to say a kind word.

He sat on his hill feeling the wind, watching the animals, and protecting them. He wished that he had someone to watch him, like he watched them.

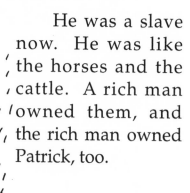

He was a slave now. He was like the horses and the cattle. A rich man owned them, and the rich man owned Patrick, too.

"I wish that I had a friend," Patrick sighed, as the cold night wind slapped at him. "I wish I could hear a kind voice and feel the warmth of love."

"I had a mother, once, who comforted me," Patrick shouted into the raw black night. "I had a father who loved me," he yelled. "Now, I have no one," Patrick said to the stars.

But of course, even on that cold hill, in the black Irish night, with the wind roaring, and the stars far away, Patrick was not alone.

And that night, as he started to sleep, he felt the warmth of love surround him and fill him. And for the first time, he felt the presence of his Great Friend.

† † †

After that night, Patrick's life changed. He was still a slave and still a shepherd. He did not look different, but he was not the same Patrick at all.

Now he had a friend to talk to, a friend to comfort him and to be with him. Now Patrick no longer felt lost and alone. He felt loved, and he was full of hope.

For six years, he lived mostly outside, watching his master's cattle. And for six years, every day and every night, he prayed and prayed and prayed.

Patrick prayed through storms. He prayed through sunshine. He prayed through the cold, and he prayed through the heat.

And day after day, his friendship grew

stronger. And Patrick grew stronger and happier and wiser.

He learned a lot about himself. The first thing he learned was that he had never cared much about God, but that God cared about him.

The second thing he learned was that God had a plan for him. Patrick did not know what the plan was, but he knew that he would not be a slave forever.

So Patrick waited and waited and waited, in the cold wind and the black Irish nights, through spring and summer and winter and fall, and spring and summer and winter and fall.

And as he waited, he met some of the Irish people, and he got to know them, and he got to like them, and he learned how to speak their language.

One night when Patrick was sleeping, God, his Great Friend, spoke to him.

"You have done well in this time of suffering. Soon you will go home."

Patrick was filled with joy and hope. And he waited and prayed and trusted, but still he wondered and wondered how and when he would go home.

And a night or two later as he slept, God answered his question.

"See," God said to Patrick, "Your ship is ready."

Patrick was far away from the sea. What the voice said seemed strange to him, but Patrick believed that it was God's voice, and so he left the cattle and started walking.

Patrick did not know where he was. He did not know where the sea was, or the harbor or the ship, but he kept on walking.

He walked up hills and down. He waded across streams, and he stumbled through forests. In fact, he walked two hundred miles.

He was a runaway slave, and as he walked, he knew he was in danger. But he trusted in the voice of his Friend, and he walked and he walked and he walked.

And then, he came down a hill and through some woods, and there it was! The great sea. And in front of him, a ship and sailors and freedom.

"At last!" Patrick cried. "At long, long last!"

And he ran to the ship, but the captain was afraid.

"Get out of here, you slave. We're not taking you on this ship," the captain shouted.

Patrick did not argue with the captain. He turned and walked away. But as he walked, he prayed. And he did not walk very far or pray very long.

"Come back," some sailors shouted, "The captain has changed his mind. Come back."

And Patrick ran to the ship and jumped on board.

"Hurry," the captain said. "Let's get out of here."

Sometimes the men were friendly, and sometimes they were ugly and mean. The captain cared more about the cargo than he cared about Patrick or the sailors.

The cargo was Irish wolf- hounds. They

were gray and big and handsome. And the captain planned to make money by selling them when the ship landed.

This time, the crossing was much better. The wind blew at their backs, the skies were clear, and the waves were gentle, and in three days, the ship had made land.

† † †

Patrick's troubles were not over yet. He was still far from home and still a captive. And the land they had come to was barren. The fields and woods had all been burned.

Patrick did not want to be where he was. He wanted to escape from these people. He wanted to go home to his parents and live in a house with a bed.

Patrick thought he might never be free. And one night he said that to God. But the Voice told him not to worry.

"Just two more months, Patrick," the Voice said.

They hunted and searched, but they could not find food. There were no towns or houses. There were only ashes and weeds.

After almost a month, they were starving. The men were weak, and the dogs were dying. The farther they went, the weaker they got, and the more angry the men and the captain became.

And they all seemed to be angry with Patrick. He had done nothing to make them angry. He had just talked about his Great Friend, Jesus, but they had not paid much attention – until now.

"If your God is so great," shouted the captain, "Ask him to get us some food."

"Why don't you ask Him with me," Patrick said.

"What?" the captain said.

"What?" the sailors said.

"My God is great," Patrick said to them. "And if you turn to Him and really ask for His help, He may send you some food. After all, there is nothing He can't do."

So Patrick and the captain and the sailors prayed. They told God that they were hungry and afraid. They said that they had no one to help them. And that if He did not help them, they would die.

As they prayed, they thought they heard thunder. Its rumbles got louder and louder and louder. They tried to keep praying, but the dogs were barking, and the thunder was so loud, they couldn't hear each other.

They stopped praying and opened their eyes. Running right at them was a great herd of pigs! They were so surprised, it took a few moments before they started tackling the pigs.

They ate and they ate and they ate. The men ate, and the dogs ate, and Patrick ate. And when they were full, they all thanked

Patrick and God.

But Patrick was still not free. Instead of being in Britain, he was in Gaul. And instead of being with his family, he was stuck with the sailors and the dogs.

Chapter Two

Among Friends

The sailors and the dogs and Patrick spent another month in the wilderness. Then at last, they came to a place where there were people and food.

Patrick was very happy. The Voice had been right again. He had seemed to be lost and alone, and now that was all over.

For the first time in more than six years, he was with people like his parents. They were kind and friendly, and they did not treat him like a slave.

The people liked Patrick, and Patrick liked them. They fed him and gave him clothes, and they even brought him to a place where he could have a bed to sleep in.

The place was a monastery where priests and monks lived. They grew their own food, and they worked, and they prayed.

Patrick fit right in at the monastery. Like the other men, Patrick worked and prayed.

He helped grow the food and cook it. And he took care of the sheep and cows.

One night, after they had eaten, Patrick told the men about his life – How he had been kidnapped from his parents, and how he had been made a slave.

He told them how God had spoken to him, and how he had escaped from Ireland. He told them about the sailors and the pigs,

and how God had been with him through it all.

Then some of the men spoke about themselves. They told

of how they wanted to serve God, and how they wanted to help others. They said that was why they became priests.

One night as they talked after dinner, an older priest looked Patrick in the eye.

"Patrick," he asked, "Do you think God may be calling you to become one of us?"

All the men looked at Patrick.

"Me?" Patrick asked,"Is God calling me to be a priest like you?"

No one answered. No one even spoke.

Patrick thought of his parents who were far away or maybe even dead. He thought of his town and his friends. And he thought of the wild, wild Irish people.

"My grandfather was a priest," Patrick said. "And my father is a deacon. But I am far away from home, and I am hardly educated at all."

"I know how to watch sheep and how to pray through the night. I have learned to live in the cold rain, but I have never learned the Bible."

"If you know that God loves you, you are very wise," the old priest said. "And you have had the best teacher of all. God, Himself, has taught you."

Patrick thought about his parents and the

terrible day he was kidnapped. He longed to see his family, and the old priest read his heart.

"Return to your people, Patrick. And spend some time with them. If God is calling you, and I think He is, come back to us."

† † †

And so after a few days, with the help and blessing of the priests, Patrick prepared to return home. "Christ go with you," they told him.

" A h , yes," Patrick said. "Christ be in front of me, and Christ be behind me. Christ be at my right side and my left. May Christ be all around me."

Chapter Three

Back Home

His parents couldn't believe it! Their son Patrick was back home. They thought he would be a slave forever and die in a strange land, among strange people.

He had changed. He was a man now, with a full beard and a mystery in his eyes. But he had come home to them. And they held a great party to celebrate.

Patrick liked being home. He liked the comfort and warmth. He spent weeks doing almost nothing. But he still prayed, and he still wondered.

Sometimes he thought about Ireland and the voices that he heard. And sometimes he thought about Gaul and what the old priest had said to him.

Ireland, Patrick thought, wasn't a bad place to visit, but he wouldn't want to live there. It was too cold and rainy, and the people, well, they were just too fierce.

Then one night, in the comfort of his bed, as he was sleeping, he had another vision. It was a vision that would change his life.

He dreamt of an angel carrying lots of letters. The angel came from Ireland, and he handed Patrick one of the letters. It began, "Voice of the Irish."

As Patrick began to read, he heard their voices. They were the people he knew when he was a slave.

"We beg you, holy young man, to come back to us and walk with us."

Patrick was deeply touched. Yet, he wondered about the dream. Who was it that was speaking to him, and what did it all mean?

He got the answer in another dream.

"The One who laid down His life for

you, is the One who speaks to you," a voice said.

And Patrick awoke filled with joy.

It was Jesus, Himself, who spoke to him. And deep down Patrick knew that Jesus was going to use him to do something wonderful.

The old priest was right. God was calling Patrick. He went to his parents and told them— It was time he went back to Gaul.

Chapter Four

Getting Ready

Years went by. Many, many years.
But Patrick did not return to
Ireland. He had other things to do
– very, very important things.

He had to study Latin, and he had to
study the Bible. He had to
learn about his Faith and
about how to be a priest.

But he never forgot
the angel who gave him
the letter. And he never
forgot the voices that

begged him to come back to Ireland.

Sometimes the memory would be dim, and sometimes it would be strong. But it was always tugging at him. It never really left him alone.

Patrick studied and prayed, and he prayed and studied. He was like an athlete who exercises to get better and better.

Athletes train their bodies, but Patrick

was training his spirit. He wanted his friendship with Jesus to grow stronger and stonger.

† † †

He was surrounded by other good
men who helped him to pray and
to learn. They showed him what it
meant to be a follower of Jesus.

He found many friends, but one young
man was special. The two of them had many
long talks, and Patrick told him all about himself.

Patrick told his friend about Ireland and
about the angel and the voices. He told his
friend about his whole life including something bad he had done.

The friend knew Patrick was a holy man,
and he admired Patrick very much. But deep
down in his heart, he was also jealous of
Patrick.

Many years passed. Patrick became a deacon, and then he became a priest. But he still did not go to Ireland.

Yet sometimes as he was falling asleep or praying, he would hear the voices.

"We beg you, holy young man, to come back to us and walk with us."

† † †

People thought so much of Patrick that after many years it was decided that Patrick should be a bishop. He would be a leader and a teacher.

"No," his friend said. "No. Don't make Patrick a bishop. He doesn't deserve to be a

bishop because he has sinned."

"But that was many years ago. That was when he was fifteen. That was before he really knew God, when he was a child," others said.

"It doesn't make any difference. Patrick shouldn't be a bishop. He's not good enough," Patrick's friend complained.

But the others knew that Peter had sinned, and Thomas had sinned, and Paul had persecuted Jesus.

Jesus had taken these sinners and made them powerful leaders. They became great apostles, and Patrick would be just like them.

Then Patrick heard Jesus speaking inside of him.

"Because you have been hurt, I have been hurt. They have tried to ruin your name. But you are special to me, and when they try to hurt you, they try to hurt the apple of my eye."

† † †

Still, Patrick wondered. It had been many years since he heard the Irish voices calling him to come back.

And when he was finally ready, another priest was made bishop and sent to Ireland to convert the wild people.

Instead of going to Ireland, Patrick found himself on the road to Rome. He was going to see the Pope. At least, that's what he thought.

But at last his time had come. The bishop to Ireland had died. And word came to Patrick that he was to be bishop to the Irish.

He had heard the voices long ago, and now he was sixty years old. Others were coming to the end of their life's work, but

Patrick was just starting his.

† † †

A saintly bishop laid hands on Patrick and made him a bishop, too. Then the old bishop blessed Patrick.

"May Christ go with you," he said.

Patrick was a brave man. He had learned to put up with suffering. Courage and a strong will were important, but he knew he needed more than that.

"Christ be before me and behind me, on my left and on my right," Patrick prayed. "May those who look at me see Christ, and may those who listen to me hear Christ."

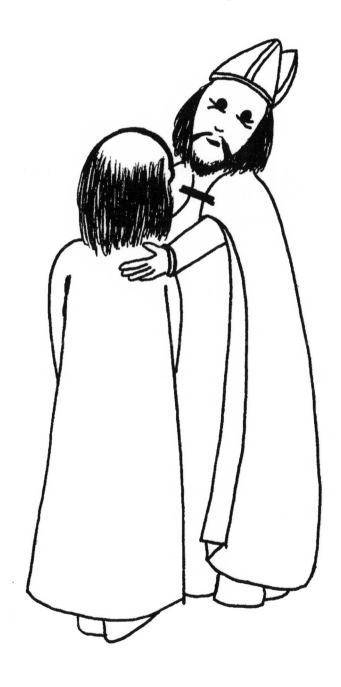

Chapter Five

The Druids

The Druids had been waiting for Patrick. They feared him without knowing him, and they hated him before they met him, because they knew he was dangerous.

The Druids ruled the wild Irish, even though they were not kings. They ruled by magic and spells, but most of all, they ruled by fear.

Years before Patrick returned to Ireland, one of the Druids had predicted that a powerful man would come across the sea and bring the Irish a new religion.

The Druids had their own religion, and they wanted Ireland for themselves. They were cruel, and they were powerful, and their gods were ugly and mean.

They planned to kill Patrick before he could bring Jesus to the Irish. That way they hoped they could keep the truth out of Ireland and out of the hearts of her people.

† † †

When Patrick landed in Ireland, he and his friends were attacked. And in order to save their lives, they got back in the boat and sailed away.

The Druids celebrated. It had been such an easy victory. Patrick had run away, they thought, but they really did not know Patrick.

Instead of going back to Gaul, he and his friends sailed up the Irish coast, because

Patrick had a plan to break the power of the Druids.

His plan was bold and daring. He would go to Tara where the high king of Ireland lived, and he would defeat the Druids.

So they sailed up a river and landed, and Patrick and his friends went up on a high hill a few miles from Tara.

It was a special night for the Druids. They were celebrating the annual change when the days start to get longer than the nights, and things begin to grow again.

It was a special night for Patrick, too. He was celebrating the vigil of Easter and the moment that changed history when Jesus was raised from the dead.

That night was most important to the Druids. There could be no light in all of Ireland until they lit a fire on the hill of Tara in honor of their mean and ugly gods.

"There is a great darkness over Ireland," Patrick said. "But we have come to bring the Light. It is the Light of Easter, the Light of Christ which will shine forever in the hearts of the Irish."

"Our Light will overcome the darkness of the Druids and of their gods. Light the Easter fire to show that Christ is risen."

On the far hill of Tara, in the great hall of the king, the powerful Druids smiled in the darkness, believing they owned the souls of the Irish.

"Oh, great king," a voice shrieked, "Someone has broken your law. There should be darkness in all the land, but a light is shining on the hill."

"It is the one from across the sea," a Druid cried.

"He must die," another shouted. "If he lives, we are finished. If he lives, he will conquer Ireland."

Then the king and the army and the Druids marched to the foot of Patrick's hill.

"Don't go to him, great king," the Druids said. "Make him come to you, and we will kill him."

† † †

Patrick came into their midst and stood without fear proclaiming Christ's rising before those who wanted to kill him.

"We have heard of your lies," a Druid shouted. "There is no Son of God. There is no Jesus. There is the power of night and the magic of spells and a spear in my hand to kill you."

"The host of God will defend me," Patrick said.

"We'll see about that," the Druid screamed.

But as he rushed to kill Patrick, he flew through the air and was smashed against a rock.

The king was in a rage.

"Grab that man," he shouted. "Shut his mouth, and stop his prayers! Do it now," the king ordered his soldiers.

But in the shadows and the darkness, the soldiers were confused, and as they tried to attack Patrick, they attacked each other instead.

The king was angry, but he was not stupid. He did not want his soldiers to harm each other. So before more damage could be done, the king decided to return to Tara.

Chapter Six

Victory

*E*aster dawned in bright beauty, on the hill where Patrick awoke and on the great hall of Tara where the king and the Druids were meeting.

And as Patrick gave thanks for the morning, the Druids cursed and plotted. And as Patrick praised the beauty of creation, the Druids cursed and planned.

"We call upon the powers of darkness, we call upon the gods of fire, we call upon murder and blood and death to fall on the head of Patrick," the Druids chanted.

"I arise today in the power of the Trinity with the power of God to guide me, the might of God to uphold me, the wisdom of God to teach me," Patrick prayed.

"We call upon the mighty powers of trees and rivers and wolves, we call forth spells and curses to capture Patrick's spirit," the Druids chanted.

"I bind myself to the power of God to

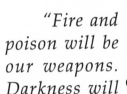

protect me from every savage power aimed at my soul or my body," Patrick prayed, "And to protect me from the spells of the Druids."

"Fire and poison will be our weapons. Darkness will

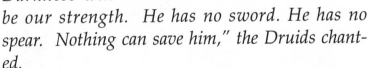

be our strength. He has no sword. He has no spear. Nothing can save him," the Druids chanted.

"Christ protect me today against poison and burning, against drowning and wounding that I may do His work."

"Christ be in front of me and inside me and behind me, Christ be above me and beneath me, at my right hand and at my left."

In the great hall at Tara they waited. The moment that they feared had come. But they were ready for it. They had spells and magic and poison.

✝ ✝ ✝

"**L**et us go to the banquet of Tara, where the Druids plan to kill us. Let us go to the great hall of the king, and let us do it without fear," Patrick said.

"For we go in the power of the Trinity, with the very might of Christ. And as sure as the first Easter changed the world, this Easter will change Ireland."

✝ ✝ ✝

He entered the hall without a weapon and without being invited. When they saw him before the king, a great quiet fell over the place.

No eye left him and every ear waited for his words.

"I come to bring wonderful news to Ireland. I have come to tell you of your savior who will free you from death and from darkness."

† † †

(That morning has been hidden by history and by the tales of the Irish poets, and no one is sure what happened next. But we do know that something miraculous took place.

And since legends are not without honor, especially when they have lasted so long, let us hear what the legends say about what happened at Tara that morning.)

† † †

The chief Druid jumped to his feet. "Before you tell us your news, you must follow our custom, and share a drink with us," he said.

He walked to Patrick and gave him a cup, and everybody in the hall knew it was poisoned. But Patrick took the cup and blessed it, and then he drank it down in one gulp.

"I have come to tell you of Jesus Christ, the Son of God, who died for your sins, who was raised up by the power of the Holy Spirit, and who offers you eternal life," Patrick said.

"There is no power that can raise the dead. But even if there was, we have greater power than Jesus or this spirit you speak of," the Druid said, "And we certainly have greater power than you."

Patrick turned to the king.

"If this man is right, and we are wrong then do what you want with us. But if we are right, then grant my wish."

"And what is your wish?" the king asked.

"I wish to go the length and breadth of Ireland. I wish to teach the people and baptize them. I wish to free this land from the dark spirits."

"You have my word," the king promised Patrick, "If you are more powerful than the Druids, and your God is more powerful than their magic, then you are free to travel all of Ireland."

"Let us have a trial by fire," the Druid priest said.

"Let us have whatever trial you want,"

Patrick replied.

"We will build two straw houses," the Druid said, "With your man in one and my man in the other."

"That sounds just fine to me," Patrick said.

"But we will put your cloak around my man and my cloak around yours," the Druid said.

"Then do it," Patrick said.

"Let me have the Druid's cloak," said one of Patrick's friends. "Just so long as you pray over me, Patrick," he said as he stepped into a straw house.

A trembling Druid stepped before Patrick, and the Bishop of Ireland gave him his cloak. The Druid wrapped himself in the great garment and stepped into the other straw house.

As Patrick prayed, the Druids set the houses on fire. And as Patrick prayed, screams filled the hall. As Patrick prayed, the Druids sneered and cursed him, and as Patrick prayed, the fires burned themselves out.

The Druid priest kicked away the embers, and there untouched was Patrick's cloak. But the Druid's man was

burnt to ashes.

"Where is your power now?" Patrick asked.

"And where is yours?" the Druid asked.

He kicked away the embers of the other straw house and smiled when he saw his cloak had been burnt to ashes.

"And where is your power now?" the Druid asked.

"It is right here," Patrick answered, as his man stepped from the ashes. "But it is not my power," Patrick said. "It is the power of the Trinity."

† † †

(Perhaps that's the way it happened, or nearly the way it happened. Or perhaps it was even something more wonderful that took place in Tara's great hall that morning.)

† † †

A great quiet fell over the place, and every eye was on Patrick as he stood before the king. "I have come to tell you of your savior who will free you from death and from darkness."

The Druids mocked and sneered, trying to keep him from being heard. Patrick looked at the king and waited.

"Be quiet," the king ordered the Druids.

The king's words shocked the Druids, and an awe filled the great hall. Patrick bowed to the king and turned to the people.

"Men and women of Ireland, listen to

God's word.

"You are a people rich in courage. You are a proud and noble race. But you live in darkness, and you die in darkness. And it is time for you to come into the light.

"The God who created the universe, who made this island and the sea around it, wants to make you His sons and daughters, and He has sent me as His messenger.

"No longer must you kill each other or sacrifice your children. No longer must you live in fear of the Druids and their spells.

"The Father of us all has sent His Son to free you from sin and give you His Spirit."

When Patrick stopped speaking, a terrific hush fell on them all.

Some stood in silence, others wept, but every man, woman and child was touched.

On that fateful Easter morning, the Irish heard the Word of God, and they took it to their hearts and held it fast.

† † †

When Patrick left the great hall that day, the course of Irish history was changed. He had received the king's permission to preach and teach throughout the land.

Because of Patrick's work, love and learning replaced fierceness. And Ireland, which had been so feared, became known as the Island of Saints and Scholars.

So God blessed the Irish by sending them Patrick. And He blessed a lot of other people – By sending them the Irish.

† † †

Events are not always written down. So history is incomplete. And sometimes the spaces in history are filled by stories repeated for centuries.

It is said that as Patrick walked down the hill from Tara, the Irish asked about the Trinity. How could there be one God in three?

Patrick saw a shamrock growing on the hill, and he picked it up and showed them.

"It's three in one, and one in three, sort of like this shamrock," Patrick said.

And of course everyone knows Patrick drove the snakes from Ireland. Though some say there never were any snakes there. Unless you think of the Druids as snakes.

† † †

So we come to the end of our story of Patrick although Patrick's story has never ended. The Faith he planted in Ireland fifteen centuries ago is flowering throughout the world today.

The boy who became a slave, returned as a bishop to Ireland. And God Blessed the Irish – and He has kept blessing them ever since.

The End
(but there's more)

Patrick's Prayer

The Deer's Cry

I arise today
Through a mighty strength, the invocation of
    the Trinity,
Through a belief in the Threeness,
Through confession of the Oneness
Of the Creator of creation.

I arise today
Through the strength of Christ's birth and His
    baptism,
Through the strength of His crucifixion and
    His burial,
Through the strength of His resurrection and
    His ascension,
Through the strength of His descent for the
    judgment of doom.

I arise today
Through the strength of the love of cherubim,
In obedience of angels,
In service of archangels,
In the hope of resurrection to meet with reward,
In the prayers of patriarchs,
In preachings of the apostles,
In faiths of confessors,
In innocence of virgins,
In deeds of righteous men.

I arise today
Through the strength of heaven;
Light of the sun,
Splendor of fire,
Speed of lightning,
Swiftness of the wind,
Depth of the sea,
Stability of the earth,
Firmness of the rock.

I arise today
Through God's strength to pilot me;
God's might to uphold me,
God's wisdom to guide me,
God's eye to look before me,
God's ear to hear me,

God's word to speak for me,
God's hand to guard me,
God's way to lie before me,
God's shield to protect me,
God's hosts to save me
From snares of the devil,
From temptations of vices,
From every one who desires me ill,
From far and from near,
Alone or in a mulitude.

I summon today all these powers between me
        and evil,
Against every cruel merciless power that
        opposes my body and soul,
Against incantations of false prophets,
Against black laws of pagandom,
Against false laws of heretics,
Against craft of idolatry,
Against spells of women and smiths and wizards,
Against every knowledge that corrupts man's
body and soul.

Christ shield me today
Against poison, against burning,
Against drowning, against wounding,
So that reward may come to me in abundance.

Christ with me, Christ before me, Christ
        behind me,
Christ in me, Christ beneath me, Christ above me,
Christ on my right, Christ on my left,
Christ when I lie down, Christ when I sit down,
Christ in the heart of every man who thinks of me,
Christ in the mouth of every man who speaks
        of me,
Christ in the eye that sees me,
Christ in the ear that hears me.

I arise today
Through a mighty strength, the invocation of
        the Trinity,
Through a belief in the Threeness,
Through a confession of the Oneness
Of the Creator of creation.

Ambassador Books, Inc.

Spiritus et Veritas

OUR MISSION

The publishing world has changed dramatically in the last few decades. Prominent houses have been taken over by larger corporations which are driven by a bottom-line mentality. The result has been an industry-wide trend to reach the widest possible audience. This in turn has led to a marketing strategy which promotes the mediocre and the superficial.

In fiction, this means a nation which once supported Faulkner, Fitzgerald, Hemingway, Steinbeck, O'Hara, O'Neill, and Miller now chooses from a long list of best sellers conspicuous for its lack of substance. In the areas of philosophy, theology and psychology, we study the occult and self-help books. As writers, only our historians are first-rate. It is an irony of some magnitude that as science has made unparalleled progress by objective, empirical examination of physical reality, the examination of spiritual reality has become subjective and truth has become arbitrary and transient.

There is a tremendous void in publishing. It has lost touch with the human appetite for excellence and for art.

The purpose of Ambassador Books is to serve a readership which is now largely ignored. Our mandate is to produce and market intellectually and spiritually stimulating books which have substance and depth.

Our standard will be excellence. Our works will be well-written, well-edited and well-designed. We will use good materials to produce quality products providing good value in every sense of the term to our readers.

We believe Western Civilization is due for another renaissance. Our aim is to help promote that.

And God Blessed the Irish -- The Story of Patrick is the first in a series of children's books about saints. The second will be *God's Little Flower -- Therese of Lisieux.*

Ambassador Books, Inc.
71 Elm Street
Worcester, MA 01609

To order, call: 800 577-0909

This is a photograph of the Celtic Cross located on the north side of City Hall in Worcester, Massachusetts. It also appears on the cover.